Crochet Jewelry
20 Crochet Bracelets, Earrings, and Rings
You Can Make Yourself!

2

Table of content

Introduction

Every day is a good day to set a new trend, and you are always ready to strut your stuff. But, this isn't always easy when you have a limited selection of items to choose from.

Sure, you can mix and match, but how many times can you do that without being bored? You want something new and exciting. You want something that makes you feel amazing as you walk down the street, and you want something that is going to show the world that you know how to set trends, and you aren't afraid to do it.

But, you feel overwhelmed.

Where do you start?

How do you know you are going to get the pieces that you want?

How to you express your style when you feel like you've hit a creative roadblock?

If you have been feeling this way, you have come to the right place. In this book, you are going to learn everything you need to know to create your own jewelry pieces, and to show off to the world your own unique style. Whether you choose to make these each as they are exactly, or you take what you see here and turn them into something that is your own, you are going to find that making your own jewelry line is easier than ever.

This book is going to give you everything you need to crochet your own jewelry pieces, and you are going to find the inspiration to be endless. So go ahead, put on your own creative thinking cap, and get ready to dive into a new world of jewelry and trends like you have never imagined before.

There's no way you can do it wrong when you are happy with the results, and this book is the little push you need to get there. Settle in with your favorite crochet hook, your favorite color yarn, and a glass of your favorite ice cold beverage, and you are going to get everything you have ever wanted for your accessory collection.

Get ready to dive into the world of fashion design, and learn for yourself what it feels like to create pieces that you are happy to show off to the world. You know you want to, so don't let anything hold you back.

Let's get started.

Chapter 1 – Crochet Earrings

Red as a Ruby Dangle Earrings

Photo made by: kaylkels

You will need:

Earring hooks

Size E crochet hook

Needle and thread

Jewelry wire

Thread yarn

Directions:

Chain 14 and join with a slip stitch to form a ring.

Single crochet in the center of this ring 16 times, and join with a slip stitch. Chain 1, turn, and single crochet back to the other side. Join with a slip stitch. Chain 1, turn, and single crochet back to the beginning. Join with a slip stitch.

Continue until you are happy with the size of the earring, then finish with a border.

To shape the petals, you are going to:

Chain 3 and skip the first 2 stitches, then join with a slip stitch in the next stitch. Chain 3 and skip the next 2 stitches, then join with a slip stitch in the next stitch. Chain 3 and skip the next 2 stitches, and join with a slip stitch in the next stitch. Repeat around.

Repeat for the other earring.

To assemble:

Using the photo as a reference, assemble your earrings as you see here. Use tight, even stitches as you work, ensuring that none of the wire shows through the piece.

Tie off, and cut off all the loose threads. That's it!

Key Lime Earring Set

Photo made by: moiracrochetsplarn

You will need:

Earring hooks

Size E crochet hook

Needle and thread

Cross Beads

Thin lengths of plastic in the color of your choice (cut up plastic bags work well)

Directions:

Chain 4 and join with a slip stitch to form a ring.

Single crochet in the center of this ring 8 times, and join with a slip stitch. Chain 1, turn, and single crochet back to the other side. Join with a slip stitch. Chain 1, turn, and single crochet back to the beginning. Join with a slip stitch. Chain 1, turn, and single crochet back to the other side.

Continue until you are happy with the size of the earring, then finish with a border.

Repeat for the other earring.

To assemble:

Using the photo as a reference, assemble your earrings as you see here. Use tight, even stitches as you work, ensuring that none of the wire shows through the piece. Attach the beads as you see in the photo as well.

Tie off, and cut off all the loose threads. That's it!

All the Gum Drops Earrings

Photo made by: moiracrochetsplarn

You will need:

Earring hooks

Size E crochet hook

Needle and thread

Thin lengths of plastic in the color of your choice (cut up plastic bags work well)

Directions:

Chain 4 and join with a slip stitch to form a ring.

Single crochet in the center of this ring 8 times, and join with a slip stitch. Chain 1, turn, and single crochet back to the other side. Join with a slip stitch. Chain 1, turn, and single crochet back to the beginning. Join with a slip stitch. Chain 1, turn, and single crochet back to the other side.

Continue until you are happy with the size of the earring, then tie off.

Repeat for the other earring.

To assemble:

Using the photo as a reference, assemble your earrings as you see here. Use tight, even stitches as you work, ensuring that none of the wire shows through the piece.

Tie off, and cut off all the loose threads. That's it!

Bleeding Heart Earrings

Photo made by: <u>moiracrochetsplarn</u>

You will need:

Earring hooks

Size E crochet hook

Needle and thread

Thin lengths of plastic in the color of your choice (cut up plastic bags work well)

Directions:

13

Chain 4 and join with a slip stitch to form a ring.

Single crochet in the center of this ring 8 times, and join with a slip stitch. Chain 1, turn, and single crochet back to the other side. Join with a slip stitch. Chain 1, turn, and single crochet back to the beginning. Join with a slip stitch. Chain 1, turn, and single crochet back to the other side.

Continue until you are happy with the size of the earring, then finish with a border.

To shape the petals, you are going to:

Chain 5 and skip the first 2 stitches, then join with a slip stitch in the next stitch. Chain 5 and skip the next 2 stitches, then join with a slip stitch in the next stitch. Chain 5 and skip the next 2 stitches, and join with a slip stitch in the next stitch. Repeat around.

Repeat for the other earrings, adjusting the size according to the photo.

To assemble:

Using the photo as a reference, assemble your earrings as you see here. Use tight, even stitches as you work, ensuring that none of the wire shows through the piece.

Tie off, and cut off all the loose threads. That's it!

Hoops and Swoops Earrings

Photo made by: Maria Panayiotou

You will need:

Earring hooks

Size E crochet hook

Needle and thread

Jewelry wire

Thread weight yarn in the color of your choice

Directions:

Decide how large you want the finished piece to be, then chain a length that is equal to this measurement. Single crochet across the row. Chain 1, turn, and single crochet back to the other side. Chain 1, turn, and single crochet back to the beginning. Chain 1, turn, and single crochet back to the other side. Chain 1, turn, and single crochet back to the beginning.

You are going to continue with this until the strip that you create is large enough to wrap entirely around the wire you have chosen. When you are happy with the size, tie off.

Repeat for the other earring.

To assemble:

Using the photo as a reference, assemble your earrings as you see here. Use tight, even stitches as you work, ensuring that none of the wire shows through the piece.

Tie off, and cut off all the loose threads. That's it!

Mottled Magic Earrings

Photo made by: moiracrochetsplarn

You will need:

Earring hooks

Size E crochet hook

Needle and thread

Thin lengths of plastic in the color of your choice (cut up plastic bags work well)

Directions:

Chain 4 and join with a slip stitch to form a ring.

Single crochet in the center of this ring 8 times, and join with a slip stitch. Chain 1, turn, and single crochet back to the other side. Join with a slip stitch. Chain 1, turn, and single crochet back to the beginning. Join with a slip stitch. Chain 1, turn, and single crochet back to the other side.

Continue until you are happy with the size of the earring, then finish with a border.

To shape the petals, you are going to:

Chain 5 and skip the first 2 stitches, then join with a slip stitch in the next stitch. Chain 5 and skip the next 2 stitches, then join with a slip stitch in the next stitch. Chain 5 and skip the next 2 stitches, and join with a slip stitch in the next stitch. Repeat around.

Repeat for the other earring.

To assemble:

Using the photo as a reference, assemble your earrings as you see here. Use tight, even stitches as you work, ensuring that none of the wire shows through the piece.

Tie off, and cut off all the loose threads. That's it!

Star of the Show Earring Set

Photo made by: mccordworks

You will need:

Earring hooks

Size E crochet hook

Needle and thread

Jewelry wire

Thin lengths of plastic in the color of your choice (cut up plastic bags work well)

Directions:

Chain 4 and join with a slip stitch to form a ring.

Single crochet in the center of this ring 8 times, and join with a slip stitch. Chain 1, turn, and single crochet back to the other side. Join with a slip stitch. Chain 1, turn, and single crochet back to the beginning.

Continue until you are happy with the size of the earring, then finish with a border.

To shape the petals, you are going to:

Chain 5 and skip the first 2 stitches, then join with a slip stitch in the next stitch. Slip stitch down the side of the circle until you are ready to form another point. Chain 5 and skip the next 2 stitches, then join with a slip stitch in the next stitch.

Slip stitch down the side of the piece until you are ready to make another point. Chain 5 and skip the next 2 stitches, and join with a slip stitch in the next stitch.

Repeat around. When you are finished, tie off.

Repeat for the other earring.

To assemble:

Using the photo as a reference, assemble your earrings as you see here. Use tight, even stitches as you work, ensuring that none of the wire shows through the piece.

Tie off, and cut off all the loose threads. That's it!

Chapter 2 – Crochet Bracelets

Sea Bracelet

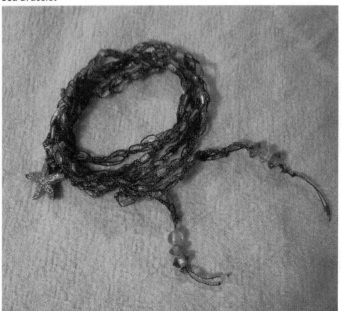

Photo made by: <u>wisewellwoman</u>

What you will need:

Size E crochet hook

Beads

Charms

Needle and thread

Thread weight yarn of your choice

Directions:

Decide how large you want the finished piece to be, then chain a length that is equal to this measurement. Single crochet across the row. Chain 1, turn, and single crochet back to the other side.

This is going to remain a thin length of chain, as you are going to then wrap it around the beads you have selected. After you are happy with how long and thick the first piece is, and you know it's going to fit the beads, you are going to tie off and set it aside.

Chain another length that is equal to the first. Single crochet across the row. Chain 1, turn, and single crochet back to the other side.

Once again, this is going to remain a thin length of chain, as you are going to then wrap it around the beads you have selected. After you are happy with how long and thick the first piece is, and you know it's going to fit the beads, you are going to tie off and set it aside.

Once more, chain another length that is equal to the first. Single crochet across the row. Chain 1, turn, and single crochet back to the other side.

When you have finished the three chains, you are ready to assemble.

To assemble:

Use the photo as a reference for assembly, and don't be afraid to throw in some of your own creativity. Intertwine the pieces together, make sure they are all secure, and attach any and all charms that you wish to be on your piece.

When you are happy with how it looks, snip off any loose ends, and attach a clasp, if desired.

That's it!

It's All in the Braid

Photo made by: <u>tafkabecky</u>

What you will need:

Size E crochet hook

Needle and thread

Thread weight yarn of your choice

Directions:

Decide how large you want the finished piece to be, then chain a length that is equal to this measurement. Single crochet across the row. Chain 1, turn, and single crochet back to the other side.

This is going to remain a thin length of chain, as you are going to braid them together when you are done. After you are happy with how long and thick the first piece is, you are going to tie off and set it aside.

Chain another length that is equal to the first. Single crochet across the row. Chain 1, turn, and single crochet back to the other side.

Once again, this is going to remain a thin length of chain, as you are going to braid them together when you are done. After you are happy with how long and thick the first piece is, you are going to tie off and set it aside.

Once more, chain another length that is equal to the first. Single crochet across the row. Chain 1, turn, and single crochet back to the other side.

When you have finished the three chains, you are ready to assemble.

To assemble:

Use the photo as a reference for assembly, and don't be afraid to throw in some of your own creativity. Intertwine the pieces together, make sure they are all secure, and attach any and all charms that you wish to be on your piece.

When you are happy with how it looks, snip off any loose ends, and attach a clasp, if desired.

And you are done!

The Cage of Glory Bracelet

Photo made by: <u>moiracrochetsplarn</u>

What you will need:

Size E crochet hook

Thin plastic strips – cutting up a plastic bag works well.

Needle and thread

Directions:

Chain 12.

Single crochet across the row. Chain 16 now, and join with a slip stitch to the opposite side of the bracelet. Single crochet in the first stitch. Chain 16 once more, and join with a slip stitch to the other side of the bracelet. Single crochet in the first stitch.

Continue until the bracelet can fit around your wrist, then assemble.

To assemble:

Use the photo as a reference for assembly, and don't be afraid to throw in some of your own creativity. Intertwine the pieces together, make sure they are all secure, and attach any and all charms that you wish to be on your piece.

When you are happy with how it looks, snip off any loose ends, and attach a clasp, if desired.

That's it! You're done!

It's Hip to be a Square

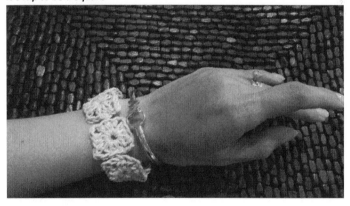

Photo made by: tracey leigh

What you will need:

Size E crochet hook

Thread weight yarn in the color of your choice

Needle and thread

25

Directions:

Chain 4 and join with a slip stitch to form a ring.

Single crochet in the center of this ring 8 times, and join with a slip stitch. Chain 1, turn, and single crochet back to the other side. Join with a slip stitch. Chain 1, turn, and single crochet back to the beginning. Join with a slip stitch. Chain 1, turn, and single crochet back to the other side.

Continue until you are happy with the size of the center.

To form the square shape, you are going to single crochet across the top, then chain 3 before continuing to single crochet in the very next stitch. This will form the angle. Single crochet across the side and chain 3 to form the next angle. Repeat for the other two sides.

Work 1 more row of single crochet, following your new pattern. Tie off and repeat until you have enough squares to fit around your wrist.

To assemble:

Use the photo as a reference for assembly, and don't be afraid to throw in some of your own creativity. Intertwine the pieces together, make sure they are all secure, and attach any and all charms that you wish to be on your piece.

When you are happy with how it looks, snip off any loose ends, and attach a clasp, if desired.

That's it, your new bracelet is ready for anything!

The Simple Solution

Photo made by: <u>mariatenorio</u>

What you will need:

Size E crochet hook

Thread weight yarn in the color of your choice

Needle and thread

Directions:

Decide how large you want the finished piece to be, then chain a length that is equal to this measurement. Single crochet across the row. Chain 1, turn, and single crochet back to the other side.

This is going to remain a thin length of chain, as you are going to sew them together when you are done. After you are happy with how long and thick the first piece is, you are going to tie off and set it aside.

Chain another length that is equal to the first. Single crochet across the row. Chain 1, turn, and single crochet back to the other side.

Once again, this is going to remain a thin length of chain, as you are going to sewing it to the other strip. After you are happy with how long and thick the first piece is, you are going to tie off.

To assemble:

Use the photo as a reference for assembly, and don't be afraid to throw in some of your own creativity. Intertwine the pieces together, make sure they are all secure, and attach any and all charms that you wish to be on your piece.

When you are happy with how it looks, snip off any loose ends, and attach a clasp, if desired.

That's it!

Sunny Day Bracelet

Photo made by: <u>nikijulian</u>

28

What you will need:

Size G crochet hook

Large button

Cotton yarn in the color of your choice

Needle and thread

Directions:

Decide how large you want the finished piece to be, then chain a length that is equal to this measurement. Single crochet across the row. Chain 1, turn, and single crochet back to the other side. Chain 1, turn, and single crochet back to the beginning. Chain 1, turn, and single crochet back to the other side. Chain 1, turn, and single crochet back to the beginning.

When you are happy with how thick the strip is, you are going to tie it off. You are now ready to assemble.

To assemble:

Use the photo as a reference for assembly, and don't be afraid to throw in some of your own creativity. Intertwine the pieces together, make sure they are all secure, and attach any and all charms that you wish to be on your piece.

When you are happy with how it looks, snip off any loose ends, and attach a clasp, if desired.

That's it! You can leave it as it is, or add more buttons to it if you like, get creative!

Fall Fantasy Bracelet

Photo made by: <u>reginarioux</u>

What you will need:

Size E crochet hook

Needle and thread

Thread weight yarn in the color of your choice

Bangle wire or jewelry wire you can bend to fit your wrist

Directions:

Start with chaining a length that is as long as you want the feather to be – about 2 inches is standard. Tie off and set aside.

Next, begin chaining shorter lengths, tying each one off and setting it aside when you are happy with the size. Make the lengths that are closer to the top of the feather longer than the lengths that are at the tip, forming the feather shape.

Use the photo as reference.

To assemble:

Use the photo as a reference for assembly, and don't be afraid to throw in some of your own creativity. Intertwine the pieces together, make sure they are all secure, and attach any and all charms that you wish to be on your piece.

When you are happy with how it looks, snip off any loose ends, and attach a clasp, if desired.

That's it! Try making the bracelet over again in as many colors as you can think of!

Chapter 3 – Crochet Rings

The Simple Things Ring

Photo made by: <u>poptoplady</u>

What you will need:

Size E crochet hook

Thread weight yarn in the color of your choice

Soda caps

Needle and thread

Directions:

Chain 4 and join with a slip stitch to form a ring.

Single crochet in the center of this ring 8 times, and join with a slip stitch. Chain 1, turn, and single crochet back to the other side. Join with a slip stitch. Chain 1, turn, and single crochet back to the beginning. Join with a slip stitch. Chain 1, turn, and single crochet back to the other side.

When you are happy with the size of the center, take your soda caps and lay them as you see in the photo. You are ready to assemble.

To assemble:

Use the photo as a reference for assembly, and don't be afraid to throw in some of your own creativity. Intertwine the pieces together, make sure they are all secure, and attach any and all charms that you wish to be on your piece.

When you are happy with how it looks, take a length of thread, a crocheted chain, wire, or metal chain and cut it to the proper length to fit around your finger. Sew the main pendant of the piece to this length, and make sure you have all pieces entirely secure.

When you are happy with how it looks, you are ready to rock your new style!

The Fairy Garden Ring

What you will need:

Size E crochet hook

Thread weight yarn in the color of your choice

Needle and thread

Directions:

Chain 4 and join with a slip stitch to form a ring.

Single crochet in the center of this ring 8 times, and join with a slip stitch. Chain 1, turn, and single crochet back to the other side. Join with a slip stitch. Chain 1, turn, and single crochet back to the beginning. Join with a slip stitch. Chain 1, turn, and single crochet back to the other side.

Continue until you are happy with the size of the earring, then finish with a border.

To shape the petals, you are going to:

Chain 4 and skip the first 2 stitches, then join with a slip stitch in the next stitch. Chain 4 and skip the next 2 stitches, then join with a slip stitch in the next stitch. Chain 4 and skip the next 2 stitches, and join with a slip stitch in the next stitch. Repeat around.

To assemble:

Use the photo as a reference for assembly, and don't be afraid to throw in some of your own creativity. Intertwine the pieces together, make sure they are all secure, and attach any and all charms that you wish to be on your piece.

When you are happy with how it looks, crochet a length that will fit around your finger. Single crochet across the row. Chain 1, turn, and single crochet back to the beginning. Chain 1, turn, and single crochet back to the other side. Chain 1, turn, and single crochet back to the beginning.

Continue until you are happy with how the wrap looks around your finger, then tie off. You can make this as thin or as thick as you like.

When you are happy with how it looks, you are ready to rock your new style!

Barely There White Ring

Photo made by: anniehp

What you will need:

Size E crochet hook

Thread weight yarn in the color of your choice

36

Needle and thread

Directions:

Chain 4 and join with a slip stitch to form a ring.

Single crochet in the center of this ring 8 times, and join with a slip stitch. Chain 1, turn, and single crochet back to the other side. Join with a slip stitch. Chain 1, turn, and single crochet back to the beginning. Join with a slip stitch. Chain 1, turn, and single crochet back to the other side.

Continue until you are happy with the size of the earring, tie off.

To assemble:

Use the photo as a reference for assembly, and don't be afraid to throw in some of your own creativity. Intertwine the pieces together, make sure they are all secure, and attach any and all charms that you wish to be on your piece.

When you are happy with how it looks, take a length of thread, a crocheted chain, wire, or metal chain and cut it to the proper length to fit around your finger. Sew the main pendant of the piece to this length, and make sure you have all pieces entirely secure.

When you are happy with how it looks, you are ready to rock your new style!

The Oversized Statement Ring

Photo made by: sionakaren

What you will need:

Size E crochet hook

Thread weight yarn in the color of your choice

Needle and thread

Directions:

Chain 4 and join with a slip stitch to form a ring.

Single crochet in the center of this ring 8 times, and join with a slip stitch. Chain 1, turn, and single crochet back to the other side. Join with a slip stitch. Chain 1, turn, and single crochet back to the beginning. Join with a slip stitch. Chain 1, turn, and single crochet back to the other side.

Continue until you are happy with the size of the earring, then finish with a border.

To shape the petals, you are going to:

Chain 10 and skip the first 2 stitches, then join with a slip stitch in the next stitch. Chain 10 and skip the next 2 stitches, then join with a slip stitch in the next stitch. Chain 10 and skip the next 2 stitches, and join with a slip stitch in the next stitch. Repeat around.

To assemble:

Use the photo as a reference for assembly, and don't be afraid to throw in some of your own creativity. Intertwine the pieces together, make sure they are all secure, and attach any and all charms that you wish to be on your piece.

When you are happy with how it looks, take a length of thread, a crocheted chain, wire, or metal chain and cut it to the proper length to fit around your finger. Sew the main pendant of the piece to this length, and make sure you have all pieces entirely secure.

When you are happy with how it looks, you are ready to rock your new style!

The Plum Summer Ring

What you will need:

Size E crochet hook

Thread weight yarn in the color of your choice

Needle and thread

Directions:

Chain 4 and join with a slip stitch to form a ring.

Single crochet in the center of this ring 8 times, and join with a slip stitch. Chain 1, turn, and single crochet back to the other side. Join with a slip stitch. Chain 1, turn, and single crochet back to the beginning. Join with a slip stitch. Chain 1, turn, and single crochet back to the other side.

Continue until you are happy with the size of the earring, then finish with a border.

To shape the petals, you are going to:

Chain 4 and skip the first 2 stitches, then join with a slip stitch in the next stitch. Chain 4 and skip the next 2 stitches, then join with a slip stitch in the next stitch. Chain 4 and skip the next 2 stitches, and join with a slip stitch in the next stitch. Repeat around.

To assemble:

Use the photo as a reference for assembly, and don't be afraid to throw in some of your own creativity. Intertwine the pieces together, make sure they are all secure, and attach any and all charms that you wish to be on your piece.

When you are happy with how it looks, take a length of thread, a crocheted chain, wire, or metal chain and cut it to the proper length to fit around your finger. Sew the main pendant of the piece to this length, and make sure you have all pieces entirely secure.

When you are happy with how it looks, you are ready to rock your new style!

Oh So Tiny Ring

Photo made by: nicasaurusrex

What you will need:

Size E crochet hook

Thread weight yarn in the color of your choice

Needle and thread

Directions:

Chain 4 and join with a slip stitch to form a ring.

Single crochet in the center of this ring 4 times, and join with a slip stitch. Chain 1, turn, and single crochet back to the other side. Join with a slip stitch. Chain 1, turn, and single crochet back to the beginning.

Continue until you are happy with the size of the earring, then finish with a border.

To shape the petals, you are going to:

Chain 3 and skip the first stitch, then join with a slip stitch in the next stitch. Chain 3 and skip the next stitch, then join with a slip stitch in the next stitch. Chain 3 and skip the next stitch, and join with a slip stitch in the next stitch. Repeat around.

To assemble:

Use the photo as a reference for assembly, and don't be afraid to throw in some of your own creativity. Intertwine the pieces together, make sure they are all secure, and attach any and all charms that you wish to be on your piece.

When you are happy with how it looks, take a length of thread, a crocheted chain, wire, or metal chain and cut it to the proper length to fit around your finger. Sew the main pendant of the piece to this length, and make sure you have all pieces entirely secure.

When you are happy with how it looks, you are ready to rock your new style!

Conclusion

There you have it, everything you need to know about making your own crochet jewelry, and a variety of patterns you can choose from to rock your style today. I hope this book is able to inspire you to create your very own jewelry collection, and that you take what you have learned here and create all kinds of pieces for your accessory needs.

There is no end to the ways you can create your own jewelry, or to how you can express your creativity while you do it. Have fun, show off your skills, and wow your friends and family with your new accessories every time you see them.

You know you want to, and now it's never been easier to do that very thing. You can be a fashion designer, you can get exactly what you want, when you want it, and you can do it all on your own.

Good luck!

Made in United States
Orlando, FL
24 August 2023

36336301R00026